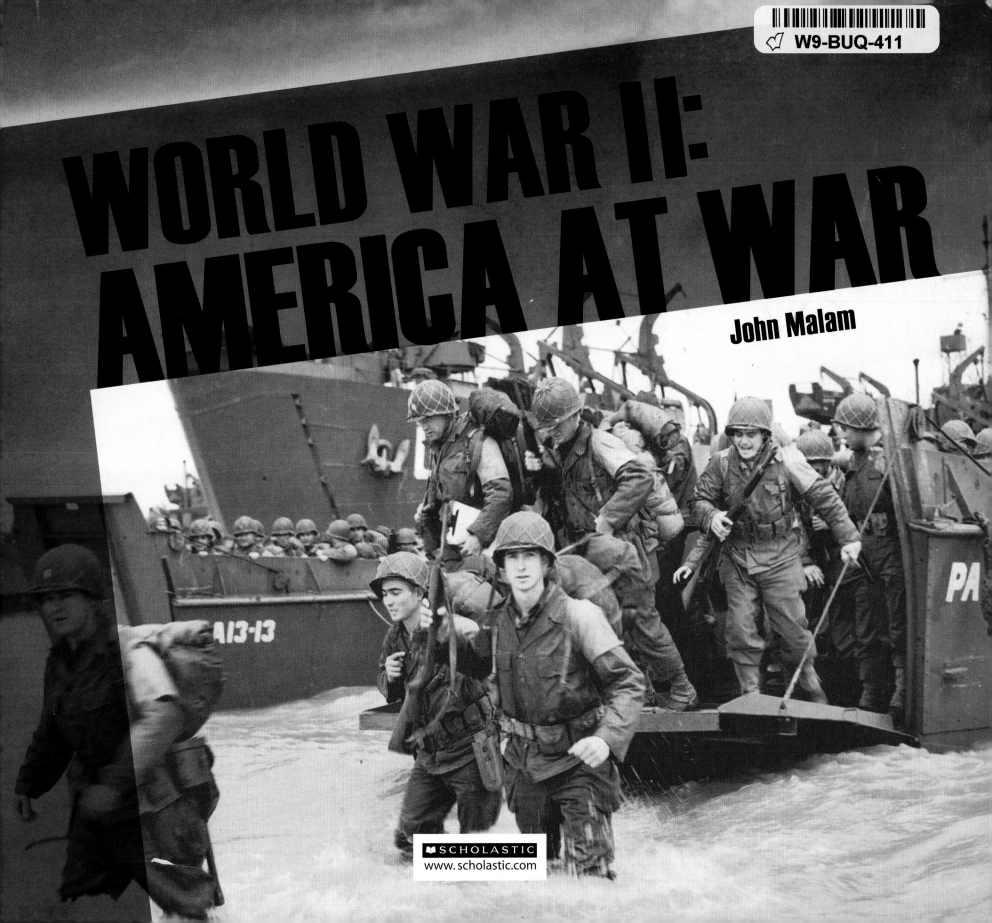

WORLD WAR II: AMERICA AT WAR

John Malam

SCHOLASTIC
www.scholastic.com

WORLD WAR II
AMERICA AT WAR

This map shows the world in 1942, after America had entered the war, with the countries and areas under the control of the **Allies** and the **Axis Powers**. Some of the key U.S. World War II campaigns and battles from 1942 to 1945 that are covered by this book are also shown.

CANADA

UNITED STATES
OF AMERICA

West Indies

 Hawaiian Islands

VENEZUEL

COLOMBIA

ECUADOR

BRA

PERU

BOLIVIA

CHILE

ARGENTIN

U.S. CAMPAIGNS AND BATTLES

1. **Pearl Harbor:** December 7, 1941
2. **Battle of the Coral Sea:** May 4–8, 1942
3. **Battle of Midway:** June 4–7, 1942
4. **Invasion of Sicily:** July 9–August 17, 1942
5. **Guadalcanal campaign (Solomon Islands):** August 7, 1942–February 9, 1943
6. **Operation Torch:** November 8–16, 1942
7. **Invasion of Italy:** September 3–16, 1943
8. **Battle of Tarawa (Gilbert Islands):** November 20–23, 1943
9. **Operation Overlord (D-Day and Normandy):** June 6–August 25, 1944
10. **Marianas campaign:** June 15–August 10, 1944
11. **Rhineland campaign:** September 15, 1944–March 21, 1945
12. **Philippines campaign:** October 20, 1944–August 15, 1945
13. **Battle of the Bulge:** December 16, 1944–January 25, 1945
14. **Battle of Iwo Jima:** February 19–March 26, 1945
15. **Battle of Okinawa:** April 1–June 22, 1945

Allies

Axis Powers

Neutral

Countries occupied or controlled by the Axis Powers

Limit of Japanese control in the Pacific

2

STEPS TO WAR: EUROPE

Wars don't usually start without any warning. They are often the result of a slow buildup of tension. This is true for World War II. The first fighting of the war was in September 1939 in Europe, but the journey to war had actually begun twenty years earlier, at the end of World War I (the Great War).

THE RISE OF HITLER

Adolf Hitler, born in Austria in 1889, fought for Germany in the Great War. Afterward, Hitler settled in Munich, where he became active in German politics. In 1920, he formed the National Socialist German Workers' Party. It soon became known as the Nazi Party, and Hitler was its leader. Millions of Germans joined the Nazi Party, believing that Hitler would make Germany a great nation once again. His power increased and in 1933 he became chancellor—the leader of the German government. In reality, Hitler was a **dictator**, whom the German people called "**Führer**" (leader).

AFTER WORLD WAR I

World War I lasted from 1914 to 1918 and was the first modern global war. More than 100 nations had been involved and when it finally ended, the victors—France, Britain, and America—drew up the Treaty of Versailles. This treaty punished Germany for the war. It limited the German Army to no more than 100,000 troops, the German Navy to no more than six warships, and the German Air Force was forbidden to have any military planes. In addition, Germany was to return land to France and the nation of Poland was set free from German control. Peacekeeping troops were to be stationed on German soil (in the Rhineland area), and Germany had to pay compensation for war damage.

A German protest against the **Treaty** of Versailles. Many Germans felt the treaty was too harsh.

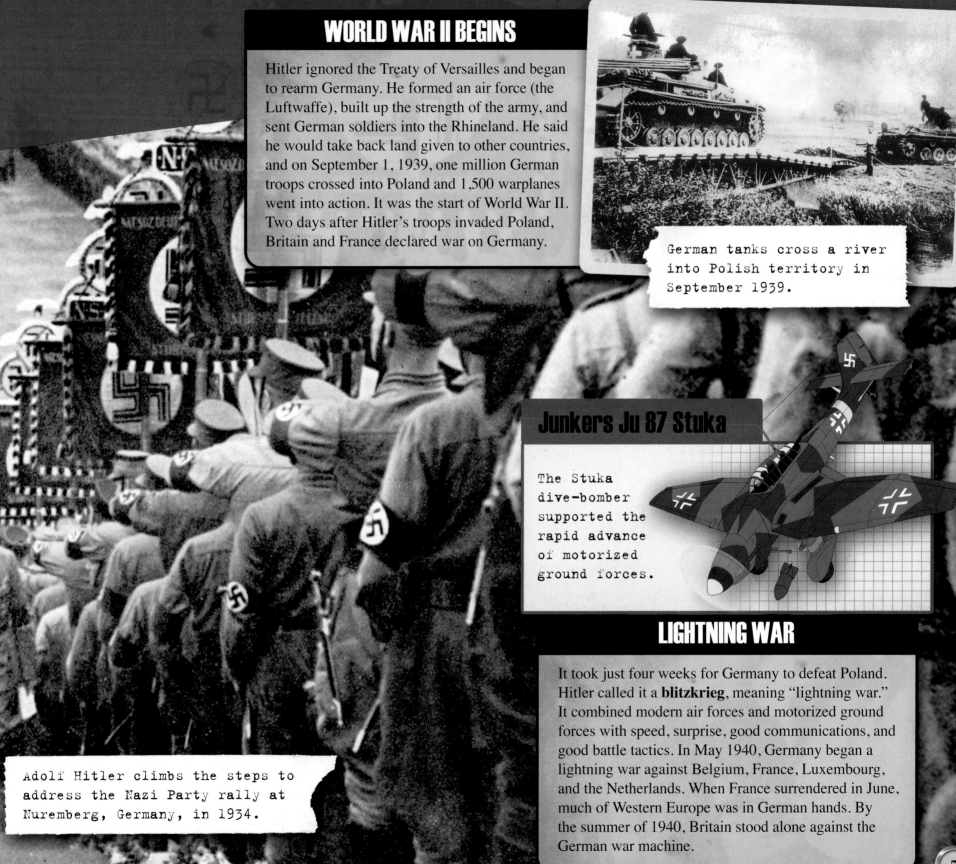

WORLD WAR II BEGINS

Hitler ignored the Treaty of Versailles and began to rearm Germany. He formed an air force (the Luftwaffe), built up the strength of the army, and sent German soldiers into the Rhineland. He said he would take back land given to other countries, and on September 1, 1939, one million German troops crossed into Poland and 1,500 warplanes went into action. It was the start of World War II. Two days after Hitler's troops invaded Poland, Britain and France declared war on Germany.

German tanks cross a river into Polish territory in September 1939.

Junkers Ju 87 Stuka

The Stuka dive-bomber supported the rapid advance of motorized ground forces.

LIGHTNING WAR

It took just four weeks for Germany to defeat Poland. Hitler called it a **blitzkrieg**, meaning "lightning war." It combined modern air forces and motorized ground forces with speed, surprise, good communications, and good battle tactics. In May 1940, Germany began a lightning war against Belgium, France, Luxembourg, and the Netherlands. When France surrendered in June, much of Western Europe was in German hands. By the summer of 1940, Britain stood alone against the German war machine.

Adolf Hitler climbs the steps to address the Nazi Party rally at Nuremberg, Germany, in 1934.

STEPS TO WAR: ASIA

At the same time as Adolf Hitler was rising to power in Nazi Germany in the 1920s, tension was growing in Asia between Japan and her neighbors. Having overturned centuries of rule by warlords and powerful families, Japan had modernized and had become Asia's leading industrial nation. The Japanese people had a high standard of living, but all this was to change.

A modern production line making vehicles in Japan before the war.

THE GREAT DEPRESSION

Japan's troubles began in the late 1920s. In 1927, the country was hit by a financial crisis and many banks went out of business. Two years later came the Wall Street Crash, when the stock market on Wall Street in New York City collapsed and millions of dollars were wiped off the value of companies. The crash led to the Great Depression—a period of economic crisis that lasted throughout the 1930s. All the world's industrial powers were affected. Factories produced fewer goods, people lost their jobs, and wages were cut. Japan, along with America and the countries of Europe, was hit hard.

A U.S. newspaper leads with a headline about the Wall Street Crash.

JAPANESE EXPANSION

To make matters worse for Japan, its larger neighbor, China, was shaping up to become a rival trading power. Japan saw this as a threat to its plans to be the leading power in Asia. In 1931, Japan responded by seizing control of territory in Northeast China, an area rich in valuable raw materials such as iron and coal, which Japan wanted.

"We must be the great arsenal of democracy."
President Franklin D. Roosevelt

The signing of the Tripartite Pact in Berlin, 1940.

THE TRIPARTITE PACT

At the same time as Japan's forces were on the move in China, Japanese diplomats were busy. On September 27, 1940, they signed an agreement with Germany and Italy in which the three countries promised to support each other. Under the terms of this Tripartite Pact, Japan agreed to fight on Germany's side—if the United States entered the war on Britain's side. This agreement brought Japan and America one step closer to war.

AMERICA'S PROMISE

Three months after Japan sided with Germany, the U.S. president, Franklin D. Roosevelt, spoke to the American people. On December 29, 1940, he promised to help Britain fight Germany by providing military supplies. In a famous phrase he described America as "the great **arsenal** of democracy." It meant that America had the military and industrial resources to aid the fight for freedom from dictators and oppressive regimes. It was a warning to both Germany and Japan.

Invading Japanese tanks in the Chinese port of Shanghai.

The U.S. president offered support to Britain, but America remained a neutral country.

AMERICA EDGES TOWARD WAR

America had watched from the sidelines as the nations of Europe went to war. The U.S. had stayed out of the conflict in 1939 and 1940, but then everything changed in 1941. As Germany and Japan set about creating a "new world order" in which they would be the leading nations, America found itself being pulled ever closer to war.

One of 50 old destroyers given to Britain through lend-lease.

AMERICAN AID

In March 1941, America decided to send equipment and war materials to Britain and its allies in the struggle against Hitler's Germany. Goods were also to be sent to China to help in its struggle against Japan. Later in the year, America also sent aid to help Russia combat invading German forces. The military equipment, goods, and money that the U.S. provided would only have to be paid for when the war was over. This arrangement was called "lend-lease."

A political cartoon from a U.S. newspaper shows the freezing of Japan's assets affecting Hitler's plans.

ACTION AGAINST JAPAN

In July 1941, in response to Japan's occupation of French Indochina and its pact with Germany, America froze all the Japanese assets in the U.S. This meant that Japanese money kept in America banks and goods waiting to be shipped to Japan had to stay in America. At a stroke, Japan was deprived of much-needed oil from America, which was then the world's largest exporter of oil. Japan had enough stored oil to last for about three years, but what would it do when that ran out?

A SECRET MEETING AT SEA

In August 1941, the U.S. warship USS *Augusta* and the British warship HMS *Prince of Wales* lay at anchor in Placentia Bay, Newfoundland. On board their respective ships were U.S. President Franklin D. Roosevelt and the British Prime Minister, Winston Churchill. After a few days of secret talks, the two leaders signed the Atlantic Charter. This important document brought America and Britain close together. They agreed to work toward common goals such as defeating dictators, giving people the right to choose their own government, and creating lasting peace. The Atlantic Charter clearly showed America's support for Britain.

Japan's Prime Minister, General Hideki Tojo.

Franklin D. Roosevelt and Winston Churchill at a church service during their meeting at sea.

JAPAN RESPONDS

Japan didn't wait for its oil reserves to run out. Nor did it agree to U.S. demands to pull out of China. Instead, on November 20, 1941, Japan's Prime Minister, General Hideki Tojo, gave America some demands of his own. He insisted that America should free Japan's frozen assets and stop supplying aid to China. In return, Japan would pull its forces out of southern French Indochina. However, Japan's demands were little more than a smokescreen. On November 26, while waiting for America to reply, a fleet of Japanese warships set sail for Hawaii. Japan was about to mount a surprise attack on the U.S. naval base at Pearl Harbor.

PEARL HARBOR

On December 2, 1941, a coded message was sent to the Japanese warships heading to Hawaii. It said: "Climb Mount Niitaka 1208." This was the order to commence hostilities against the United States with a surprise attack on the American fleet at Pearl Harbor.

Japanese bombers take off from the deck of a Japanese carrier.

JAPAN STRIKES

On the morning of Sunday, December 7, 1941, more than 350 Japanese fighters, bombers, and **torpedo** airplanes took off from six aircraft carriers, 200 miles north of the island of Oahu, Hawaii. Their target was the United States Pacific Fleet anchored at the U.S. naval base at Pearl Harbor, Oahu. The attack, which was planned and led by Admiral Isoroku Yamamoto, was designed to put the U.S. fleet out of action. If successful, Japan would then be free to mount attacks across Southeast Asia in an effort to become the region's major power.

TORA! TORA! TORA!

The Japanese planes reached Oahu undetected. Just before they began their attack, a coded message was sent back to the Japanese fleet. It said: "Tora! Tora! Tora!" (Tiger! Tiger! Tiger!), which meant the planes had caught the Americans totally by surprise. Some planes bombed the airfields, making it impossible for U.S. airplanes to take off. Others flew to Pearl Harbor in the the south of Oahu and attacked their primary target—the United States Pacific Fleet.

"A date which will live in infamy."
President Franklin D. Roosevelt

Mitsubishi A6M "Zero"

The Zero was a long-range, carrier-based fighter.

The battleships USS *West Virginia* and USS *Tennessee* on fire after the Japanese attack.

THE JAPANESE ZERO

The Mitsubishi A6M fighter plane—better known as the Zero—was Japan's main attack airplane during World War II. It had a top speed of 340 mph, a range of 1,600 miles, and was armed with two 20mm cannon and two ·303-inch machine guns. It could also carry two 130lb. bombs.

DAMAGE REPORT

The Japanese attack on Pearl Harbor lasted less than two hours, but it was devastating. It left 2,400 U.S. servicemen dead, more than 1,200 wounded, 19 ships sunk or damaged, and 188 aircraft destroyed. The Japanese attackers lost 29 planes and fewer than 200 servicemen.

DECLARATIONS OF WAR

On December 8, the day after the Pearl Harbor attack, following votes in the Senate and the House of Representatives, President Roosevelt signed the formal declaration of war against Japan. He gave a famous speech in which he declared December 7 to be "a date which will live in infamy." That same day, Britain declared war on Japan. Then, on December 11, Germany and Italy declared war against the U.S. World War II had now become a truly global conflict.

These American airplanes were destroyed by the attack before they could take off.

The *Los Angeles Times* reports the attack that led to war.

JAPANESE CONQUESTS

Pearl Harbor was not the only target in Japan's sights in December 1941. Within days, Japan also mounted a sudden invasion of the Philippines, where the U.S. had military bases, and attacked the British colonies of Hong Kong and Malaya. The attacks were so swift that U.S. and British forces had no chance to react.

EMPIRE-BUILDING

Japan's goal was to be the leading nation in Asia. The plan was to create what was called the Greater East Asia Co-Prosperity Sphere. To achieve this, Japan intended to free the region's countries from Western control.

THE BATTLE FOR HONG KONG

Hong Kong was a British **colony** in southern China with a military garrison of 12,000 troops from Britain, India, and Canada. The colony was told to hold out for as long as possible. However, Japanese spies had been in Hong Kong for years, sending back information on troops, weapons, and locations. When Japan invaded Hong Kong on December 8, it knew exactly how to stage an attack. The Battle of Hong Kong ended on Christmas Day 1941, when the British surrendered.

Victorious Japanese troops parade through Hong Kong in 1941.

A Japanese soldier in Bataan after the invasion of the Philippines in 1941.

Japanese soldiers in action in Malaya, January 1942.

JAPAN TAKES THE DUTCH EAST INDIES

Next to fall to Japan, in February 1942, were the oil-rich islands of the Dutch East Indies, including Java, Sumatra, Borneo, and New Guinea. By taking these important islands, Japan secured the oil reserves it needed to continue the war.

INVADING MALAYA

On the same day that Japan attacked Hong Kong, Japanese forces invaded Malaya. This part of the Malay Peninsula, a finger of land 700 miles long, was under British control. It produced rubber and tin—valuable resources needed for the British war effort. The Japanese made a swift advance, with some soldiers riding bicycles. British forces were pushed south to the island of Singapore, where they became trapped. On February 15, 1942, Singapore surrendered and 32,000 Indian, 16,000 British, and 14,000 Australian troops were taken prisoner.

Japanese naval parachutists landing during the attack on the Dutch East Indies in 1942.

THE PHILIPPINES FALL

Hours after the attack on Pearl Harbor, Japanese planes attacked U.S. bases on Luzon, the main island in the Philippines. Japanese ground forces then began to invade Luzon on December 10—57,000 troops arrived in all. Facing them were 13,000 U.S. troops and about the same number of well-trained Philippine Scouts, who were part of the U.S. Army. On May 7, 1942, after five months of fighting, U.S. forces surrendered.

DEATH MARCH

Following the fall of the Philippines, Japan took 75,000 prisoners of war—far more than they had expected. The men were marched 80 miles along the Bataan **Peninsula**. Conditions were terrible. Some prisoners died of disease; others were killed by their captors. About 600 Americans and 10,000 Filipinos died on what came to be known as the Bataan Death March.

neral Douglas MacArthur, mmander of the U.S. forces in the ilippines, escaped to Australia, ying: "I shall return."

WAR IN THE PACIFIC

In the early months of 1942, Japan's conquest of Southeast Asia seemed unstoppable. One by one, territories across Southeast Asia came under Japanese control. Japan carried out bombing raids from Ceylon (present-day Sri Lanka) in the west to Australia in the east. The Japanese called it the Great East Asia War. The Americans and their allies knew it as the Pacific War. It was fought on land and at sea.

AUSTRALIA BOMBED

With the capture of islands in the Dutch East Indies, Japan came a step closer to Australia. The threat of invasion became obvious on February 19, 1942, when Japan launched a bombing raid against Darwin in North West Australia. The plan was to knock out airstrips and damage the harbor, preventing it from being used by Australian, British, and U.S. forces. Japan carried out more air raids against northern Australia in the following months, leading the Allies to think that a full-scale invasion by ground forces was coming.

The remains of a U.S. bomber in a burned-out hangar, following a Japanese air attack.

CUTTING OFF AUSTRALIA

However, Japan wasn't planning to invade Australia—it just wanted to cut it off, so that it could not be used as a base for an Allied counterattack. To do that, Japan planned to take territories lying close to the north of Australia—Port Moresby on the island of New Guinea, together with the Solomon, New Hebrides, and New Caledonia island groups.

THE BATTLE OF THE CORAL SEA

Japan sent a strike force of warships to the Coral Sea off North East Australia. The force was made up of destroyers, cruisers, and two aircraft carriers carrying 127 planes. A smaller U.S. fleet, including the aircraft carriers USS *Yorktown* and USS *Lexington*, sailed to meet them. For four days in May 1942, the rival navies fought the war's first major sea battle.

U.S. Navy torpedo planes attack the Japanese carrier *Shoho* during the Battle of the Coral Sea.

The USS *Lexington* after being hit by Japanese torpedoes and bombs. Hours later the ship sank.

CARRIER WAR

The Battle of the Coral Sea was the first battle between aircraft carriers. The ships did not exchange fire or even come within sight of each other. Instead, ships on both sides were sunk or damaged by air strikes. There was no clear winner, but history records the Battle of the Coral Sea as a **strategic** success for the U.S. It prevented Japan from cutting Australia off and stopped Japanese expansion.

B-25 Mitchell

A U.S. B-25 Mitchell bomber from the Pacific campaign.

TARGET: JAPAN

On April 18, 1942, sixteen U.S. bombers took off from the USS *Hornet*, 700 miles east of Japan. Their target was Tokyo, the capital of Japan, plus some other Japanese cities. This first air strike on Japanese soil was commanded by Lt. Colonel James Doolittle. Although the Doolittle Raid caused little damage, it boosted **morale** in the U.S. and worried the Japanese, who had not thought that a heavy bombing raid against Japan was possible.

THE BATTLE OF MIDWAY

Just days after the Battle of the Coral Sea, a top-secret coded message to the Japanese fleet was intercepted. U.S. codebreakers at Pearl Harbor cracked it and uncovered Japan's plan to attack a target codenamed "AF" on June 4, 1942. But where was "AF"?

MIDWAY ATOLL

U.S. codebreakers had a hunch that "AF" was Midway Atoll—two tiny islands ringed by a coral reef in the middle of the North Pacific Ocean, roughly halfway between Asia and North America. They set a trap for the Japanese, sending out an uncoded radio message about problems with drinking water on the atoll. Sure enough, Japanese messages soon began reporting that there were water problems on "AF." The Japanese had set their sights on Midway because they saw the atoll as a stepping-stone for launching an attack against Hawaii. From Hawaii, the next stop would be the West Coast of the USA.

DIVERSION TACTICS

Japan's plan to attack Midway involved a separate attack, designed to distract the U.S. from the real target. In the far North Pacific are the Aleutian Islands, a chain of U.S. islands stretching out from Alaska toward Russia. A fleet of Japanese warships headed to the islands and on June 3, torpedo bombers and Zero fighters attacked a U.S. base. Meanwhile, Japan's main fleet headed to Midway.

Burning buildings in Dutch Harbor during the Japanese attack on the Aleutian Island

THE ATTACK ON MIDWAY

Knowing that Midway was Japan's real target, the U.S. Pacific Fleet had left its base at Pearl Harbor at the end of May. USS *Yorktown*, badly damaged in the Battle of the Coral Sea, had limped back to Pearl Harbor, where she had been repaired in record time. She joined the fleet, ready to take on the Japanese navy a second time. As expected by the U.S., Japan's attack on Midway came on June 4. It began with an air strike launched from Japanese carriers against Midway's U.S. air base. The planes returned to the carriers to rearm, ready for a second air strike.

Attacking Japanese planes are met with heavy antiaircraft fire from the U.S. fleet.

Douglas Dauntless

U.S. Dauntless dive-bombers made devastating attacks on the Japanese carriers at Midway.

DESTROYING THE JAPANESE CARRIERS

The U.S. fleet closed in. Long-range Devastator torpedo bombers were launched, but almost all were shot down by Japanese Zeros. The battle seemed to be going Japan's way, and orders were given to launch an air strike against the U.S. fleet. Bombs and airplanes crowded the decks of the Japanese aircraft carriers. Then, out of a clear sky, U.S. Dauntless dive-bombers swooped down and within minutes, three of Japan's four carriers were ablaze. The fourth was later caught and destroyed. The destruction of the Japanese carriers was a turning point in the Pacific War and opened the way for U.S. ground forces to prepare for the land war that was to come.

The uneven deck of the USS Yorktown following damage by Japanese aircraft during the Battle of Midway.

BATTLE OF THE ATLANTIC

For six years, from 1939 to 1945, Allied merchant ships crossing the Atlantic Ocean were the prey of German U-boat submarines. It was essential that these cargo ships, carrying food and supplies to Britain, France, and Russia, got through unharmed. The long struggle became known as the Battle of the Atlantic.

THE STRUGGLE AT SEA

The Battle of the Atlantic was not a "typical" sea battle. Navies did not line up opposite each other and aircraft carriers did not launch waves of aircraft against their enemy. Also, the battle lasted years, not hours or days. The opposing sides played a tense and deadly game of cat and mouse, with the hunted Allied merchant ships trying to slip past the German hunter submarines.

THE U-BOAT WOLF PACK

Germany calculated that if 750,000 tons of merchant shipping bound for Britain were sunk every month for a year, Britain would be forced to surrender. Germany's fleet of *Unterseebooten* (undersea boats, or U-boats) went into action. These submarines hunted in groups known as wolf packs, attacking at night. The tactics paid off and between July and October 1940, 217 merchant ships were sent to the bottom of the Atlantic. But it was not enough. Hitler gave orders that all merchant ships—regardless of nationality—were to be sunk on sight.

By the end of 1941, U-boats were sinking about 250,000 tons of merchant shipping every month.

1939–1945

SAFETY IN NUMBERS

For protection, merchant ships sailed in groups known as convoys. They were escorted by destroyers, and sailed in a zigzag pattern. It was found that the more ships there were in a convoy, the safer they were. More than 2,500 U.S. "Liberty ships" were specially built to carry goods to America's allies. In 1944, the war's largest convoy of 187 ships made it across the Atlantic safely.

USS REUBEN JAMES SUNK

In July 1941, the U.S. Navy began escorting ships carrying lend-lease goods across the Atlantic to Britain (see page 8). Although the U.S. was not at war with Germany, it was obvious whose side the U.S. was on. With tension rising between Germany and the U.S., it was inevitable that U.S. Navy ships would be attacked. On October 31, 1941, a U-boat torpedoed the USS *Reuben James* as the destroyer escorted merchant ships sailing from Newfoundland to Britain. Almost 160 U.S. servicemen were killed.

A U-boat under attack on the surface.

BEATING THE U-BOATS

The Battle of the Atlantic reached its height in 1943, when about 100 U-boats were on patrol at any given time. After this, improvements in antisubmarine warfare reduced the U-boat menace. Allied naval aircraft hunted them down from the air, while destroyers used **sonar** devices to bounce sound waves off U-boats. If a U-boat was detected, depth charges (underwater bombs) were dropped onto it. Also, because British codebreakers had cracked a top-secret German code, they could read messages and track the U-boats' positions.

An Allied convoy crossing the North Atlantic to deliver supplies to Europe.

ARMING FOR WAR

As nation went to war against nation, everyday life at home was put on hold. Everybody who was fit and able to work was expected to "do their bit" for the war effort. Factories worked around the clock to produce weapons, ammunition, vehicles, and supplies for the military.

GERMANY

Hitler had ignored the Treaty of Versailles and had been building up Germany's military strength since the early 1930s. When war started in 1939, Germany's war factories were ready. By the summer of 1941, more than 11 million German factory workers were making armaments.

Germany used slave workers and factories in captured countries.

British workers stacking shells.

BRITAIN

Britain was poorly prepared when war broke out, but its factories went straight into overdrive. In 1938, the year before the war, Britain's aircraft factories produced 3,000 warplanes. In 1940 they made five times as many, and by 1944 they were producing 26,000 planes a year.

JAPAN

Japan had been at war with China since 1937, so its factories were already geared up for war. Production was increased after the attack on Pearl Harbor in 1941. In 1944, about 14,000 fighter airplanes and 5,000 bombers were made, while four new aircraft carriers, 31 destroyers, and 37 submarines were launched.

Toward the end of the war, children had to work in Japan's war factories.

RUSSIA

Russia had the largest workforce. Its factories produced more warplanes than any other country. The record year was 1944, when 40,300 new airplanes took to the skies—almost five per hour. Tank numbers were also high, with more than 800,000 made during the course of the war.

Two women working on a Russian warplane.

Workmen review finished M4 Sherman tanks as they leave the factory.

Women working in a B-17 bomber.

WOMEN WAR WORKERS

During the war, many women worked in factories and shipyards, or farmed the land. Britain and Russia employed the largest number of women on war work—from growing food to building warplanes. After the U.S. entered the war, more than six million American women volunteered to help with the nation's war effort. In Germany and Japan far fewer women were involved in war work. They were encouraged to stay at home to look after the family and raise children instead.

THE UNITED STATES

President Roosevelt was being accurate when he described the U.S. as "the great arsenal of democracy." From 1941–45, the U.S. produced more than 300,000 warplanes, nearly 90,000 tanks, 1,000 warships, 200 submarines, and 10 million rifles. By 1944, the U.S. was producing 40 percent of all the world's armaments.

HOME FRONT USA

Despite rationing, there were ve
few shortages. The shelves staye
full and people didn't go hungry

Unlike many other nations, the United States itself was not invaded or occupied, and its towns and cities were not targeted by bombers. People felt safe and morale was high. The war resulted in almost full employment, increased wages, and a booming economy, and it brought about the end of the Great Depression in the U.S.

RATIONING IN THE U.S.

In January 1942, less than one month after the U.S. entered the war, the government introduced rationing, which limited the amount of goods people could buy in stores. Rationing was designed to protect stocks of essential goods and to make sure that everyone got their fair share. Tires, gas, bicycles, shoes, and even clothes were rationed. As for food, coffee, sugar, meat, cheese, butter, lard, margarine, canned foods, dried fruits, and jelly were all on the list of rationed goods.

4

564043 CE

UNITED STATES OF AMERICA
OFFICE OF PRICE ADMINISTRATION

WAR RATION BOOK FOUR

Issued to _Stacy Simpson_

Complete address _1 Mc Crone Rd_

Little Falls

READ BEFOR

In accepting this book, I recognize that it
States Government. I will use it only
authorized by the Office of Price Administra

Janet St

"Void if Altered"

It is a criminal offense to violate r

OPA Form R-145

Coupons from ration books allowed people to buy restricted goods.

Posters encouraged people to grow food in their backyards.

GROW YOUR OWN
GARDEN
Be sure!

AFRICAN AMERICANS

The war saw the mass movement of African Americans, with nearly two million relocating to work in the factories of the northern and western states. In 1942, only three percent of people involved in war production were black. By 1944, the figure was eight percent and rising. The war began to break down **discrimination** between blacks and whites, setting the scene for social changes that would come in the years after the war.

New York residents entering their air-raid shelter during a drill.

FEAR OF ATTACK

Japan's attack on Pearl Harbor and its conquests across Southeast Asia raised fears of a Japanese invasion of the U.S. mainland. More than 10 million civilians joined the Office of Civilian Defense and set about preparing for bombing raids or an invasion. Some people built bomb shelters inside their homes, or in their backyards.

African Americans work alongside whites in a U.S. bomber factory.

BALLOON BOMBS

Toward the end of 1944, Japan began a bombing campaign against the West Coast of America. Instead of using airplanes, large balloons carrying explosive or **incendiary** devices were released in Japan to drift across the Pacific Ocean. About 300 made it across. Of those that reached the U.S., one exploded in Oregon in May 1945. Six people were killed—the only deaths on the U.S. mainland in World War II due to enemy action.

JAPANESE AMERICANS

The real victims of the fear that gripped America were the nation's Japanese Americans, most of whom lived on the West Coast. In February 1942, President Roosevelt declared much of the West Coast a military zone. The government moved people out of the area. About 120,000 Japanese Americans—many of whom were American citizens—were rounded up and imprisoned in relocation camps. The unfounded fear was that they would sabotage American property or spy for Japan.

Japanese Americans being relocated under U.S. Army war emergency laws.

INVADING NORTH AFRICA

The U.S. entered the war on December 8, 1941, when it declared war on Japan following the attack on Pearl Harbor. Three days later, on December 11, Germany and Italy announced that they were at war with America. President Roosevelt immediately responded by declaring war on them.

OPERATION TORCH

If Germany and Italy were to be defeated, it was clear that the Allies would have to invade Western Europe. The only question was where the attack would begin. The answer came on November 7, 1942, when more than 500 Allied ships landed 107,000 troops and thousands of tons of weapons and supplies on the beaches of Morocco and Algeria in North Africa. It was a joint U.S. and British operation codenamed "Torch," commanded by U.S. Army officer Lieutenant General Dwight D. Eisenhower. The plan was to defeat German forces in North Africa so that an invasion force could then cross the Mediterranean Sea to attack Italy.

American troops wade ashore in Algeria during Operation Torch in November 1942.

TRAPPED IN TUNISIA

British troops were already in North Africa, fighting German forces in Egypt. As they pushed west, the U.S. and British troops in Morocco and Algeria were to push east. The plan was that the German army would be trapped in the middle, in Tunisia. Hitler reacted by sending 100,000 German and 10,000 Italian reinforcements to Tunisia, where they joined up with the German army retreating from Egypt.

The German and Italian forces in North Africa were led by Field Marshal Erwin Rommel, a masterful strategist known as the Desert Fox.

The German Panzer III had a top speed of 25 mph and fired high-explosive and armor-piercing shells.

TANK WARFARE

Tank battles dominated the North African campaign, where the sandy desert was ideal for tracked vehicles. The Germans' main desert battle tank was the Panzer III, while the Allies had the American-made M4 Sherman and British Crusader tanks. Between 1940 and 1943 the Allied and Axis tank armies battled over the desert sands of North Africa.

THE GERMAN SURRENDER

It was February 1943 before the two sides finally clashed, at the Kasserine Pass, Tunisia. The German army inflicted a heavy defeat on U.S. forces, but German success was short-lived. By May, the German army was running out of oil and food, and had fought itself to a standstill. It was trapped, with its back to the sea. On May 13, 1943, the German army surrendered and nearly 250,000 soldiers were taken prisoner. The North African campaign was over, and plans for the invasion of Italy could begin.

U.S. Sherman tank speeds rough the desert, during hting with German forces Tunisia in 1942.

German soldiers surrender to a British tank in Tunisia, May 1943.

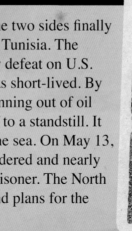

THE ITALIAN CAMPAIGN

Even before North Africa fell, the Allies had decided on their next move. That January, President Roosevelt and Winston Churchill, the British prime minister, had held a top-secret meeting codenamed "Symbol" in Casablanca, Morocco. Two major decisions were reached: to begin a bombing campaign of Germany and to invade Sicily and Italy.

OPERATION HUSKY

The operation to invade Sicily, a large island off the coast of southern Italy, was codenamed "Husky." From Sicily, the Allies planned to cross over to Italy and begin the invasion of mainland Europe. More than 2,500 troopships and landing craft crossed the Mediterranean Sea from North Africa. They carried a combined force of 180,000 U.S., British, and Canadian troops. Transport ships brought 14,000 vehicles, 600 tanks, 1,800 guns, ammunition, food, and supplies including chewing gum for the U.S. troops.

Boats are loaded with U.S. troops and equipment ready to invade Sicily.

Waco CG-4A Glider

Waco gliders were used to land Allied airborne forces during the invasion of Sicily.

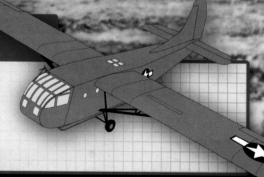

LANDING ON SICILY

The invasion of Sicily began on the night of July 9, 1943. Just before midnight, about 4,000 U.S. and British paratroopers jumped from gliders and airplanes and floated down to the island. Many drifted off course or landed far from the bridges and airfields they were meant to capture. At 2:45AM, under cover of darkness, **landing craft** began bringing the first of the Allied **infantry** troops ashore. The defending German and Italian forces were outnumbered and retreated to the port of Messina. They then escaped to Italy, just three miles across the sea. By August 12, Sicily was in Allied hands.

ITALY CHANGES SIDES

Since before the war, Italy had been led by Benito Mussolini. Like Hitler, Mussolini was a dictator. He had taken sides with Hitler against the Allies, but when Sicily was liberated, Mussolini fell from power. A new Italian government was set up and secret peace talks began with the Allies. On September 3, 1943, Italy surrendered. Hitler responded by sending German troops into Italy. Then, on October 13, 1943, Italy's new government declared war on Germany.

Allied bombing raids and food shortages contributed to Mussolini's fall from power.

THE BATTLE FOR ITALY

The same day that Italy surrendered, British forces crossed into Italy from Sicily and began to move north. Six days later, U.S. forces landed on the beaches at Salerno. The German army was waiting for them. Hitler had sent orders to stand firm, and a fierce battle was fought. After several days' fighting and with British troops approaching, the Germans retreated toward northern Italy. The U.S. and British forces gave chase and many battles were fought.

THE ROAD TO ROME

On the road to Rome, Monte Cassino was the scene of bitter fighting in the early months of 1944. At the same time, both sides fought it out on the beaches at Anzio. On June 4, 1944, the U.S. Army reached Rome and the Italian capital was **liberated**. But the German Army fought on as it retreated north. The end came on May 2, 1945, when one million German troops in Italy surrendered.

...merican soldiers during Operation ...hingle, the Allied landings at ...nzio in Italy on January 22, 1944.

The hilltop abbey at Monte Cassino was the focus of heavy fighting as the Allies battled toward Rome.

BOMBING GERMANY

The U.S. and Britain believed that the way to defeat Hitler was by intensive bombing. Britain's Royal Air Force (RAF) began bombing targets in Germany on September 4, 1939—the day after Britain declared war on Germany. After the U.S. entered the war in December 1941, United States Army Air Forces (USAAF) bombers flew from airfields in Britain on raids over Germany.

BOMBING STRATEGY

In January 1943, President Roosevelt and the British prime minister agreed to step up the bombing raids. Known as the Combined Bomber Offensive, American bombers would bomb German military and industrial targets by day and the British would do it by night. The first U.S. air strike was on January 27, 1943, when 91 B-17s and B-24s of the 8th Air Force bombed the submarine yards at Wilhelmshaven on the German North Sea coast.

An attack on a German aircraft supply factory and an aircraft repair depot in France in 1943.

OPERATION ARGUMENT

In February 1944, American and British air forces teamed up for Operation Argument. The plan was to weaken the German air force by bombing its aircraft factories. For six days, more than 3,800 U.S. and 2,300 British bombers dropped 20,000 tons of bombs on German aircraft factories. Many were put out of action for months. With fewer German planes taking to the skies, the Allies could fly deeper into Germany on long-range bombing missions. Now the Allies could invade Europe knowing that they controlled the skies.

P-51 Mustang

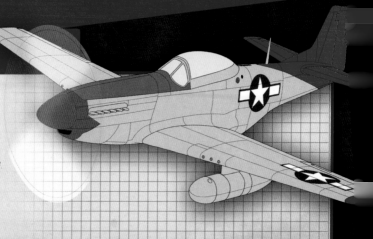

More than 15,000 Mustangs were built. They were nicknamed "Little Friends" by U.S. bomber crews.

A U.S. B-17 Flying Fortress with its bomb bay open during a raid on Germany.

ESCORT FIGHTERS

Flying alongside the B-17s were P-51 Mustangs. These single-seater U.S. fighter-bombers acted as escorts for the slower, heavier bombers. They had the same range as the bombers, but with the speed and firepower of a fighter. The P-51D Mustang flew at speeds of up to 435 mph. It had six machine guns and could carry just over 1,984lb. of bombs or six rockets.

B-17 FLYING FORTRESS

The main long-range American heavy bomber was the Boeing B-17. U.S. airmen gave it the nickname "Flying Fortress" because of its heavy armament and its ability to return from missions despite being damaged by enemy fire. On board was a crew of ten and a maximum load of 6,000lb. of bombs. With a range of 2,000 miles, the B-17 could deliver its deadly load deep inside Germany. More than 12,700 were built.

TUSKEGEE AIRMEN

During World War II, the USAAF was racially divided. If an African American wanted to become a military pilot, he was sent for training at Tuskegee Army Airfield, Alabama. Once he had earned his wings (learned to fly), he joined one of two black-only squadrons. Known as the Tuskegee Airmen, these black U.S. pilots flew Mustangs, B-25 Mitchell bombers, and other warplanes on combat missions.

Two African American airmen with an airplane at an air base at Rametti in Italy.

OPERATION OVERLORD

The bombing of Germany was the first stage of a larger plan. As factories were bombed and the Luftwaffe was destroyed, Germany started to grind to a halt. The next stage of the plan was a full-scale invasion in 1944. American, British, and Canadian ground forces would cross the English Channel from Britain and begin the invasion of northwest Europe. The invasion was codenamed "Overlord."

FALSE PLANS

To trick the Germans, **double agents** leaked false invasion plans to the Germans. Meanwhile on the southeast coast of England, fake tanks, airplanes, and landing craft were set up to make it look like an invasion force was gathering. Hitler was convinced that a fictitious force, the First United States Army Group, would land on the beaches around Calais in northern France—the closest point to Britain (about 21 miles away). He sent thousands of troops to the area, but the First United States Army Group was only a few mobile radio units sending out false messages to fool the Germans.

U.S. infantry troops on the south coast of Britain waiting to embark for the Normandy invasion.

THE REAL INVASION

Meanwhile, the real invasion force was being assembled along the south and southwest coasts of England. The plan was to land on the beaches of Normandy in northern France, far from where the Germans were expecting them. Landing craft, tanks, vehicles, and tens of thousands of soldiers were brought together in great secrecy.

One of the fake inflatable Sherman tanks used to trick the Germans. From the air, these looked like the real thing.

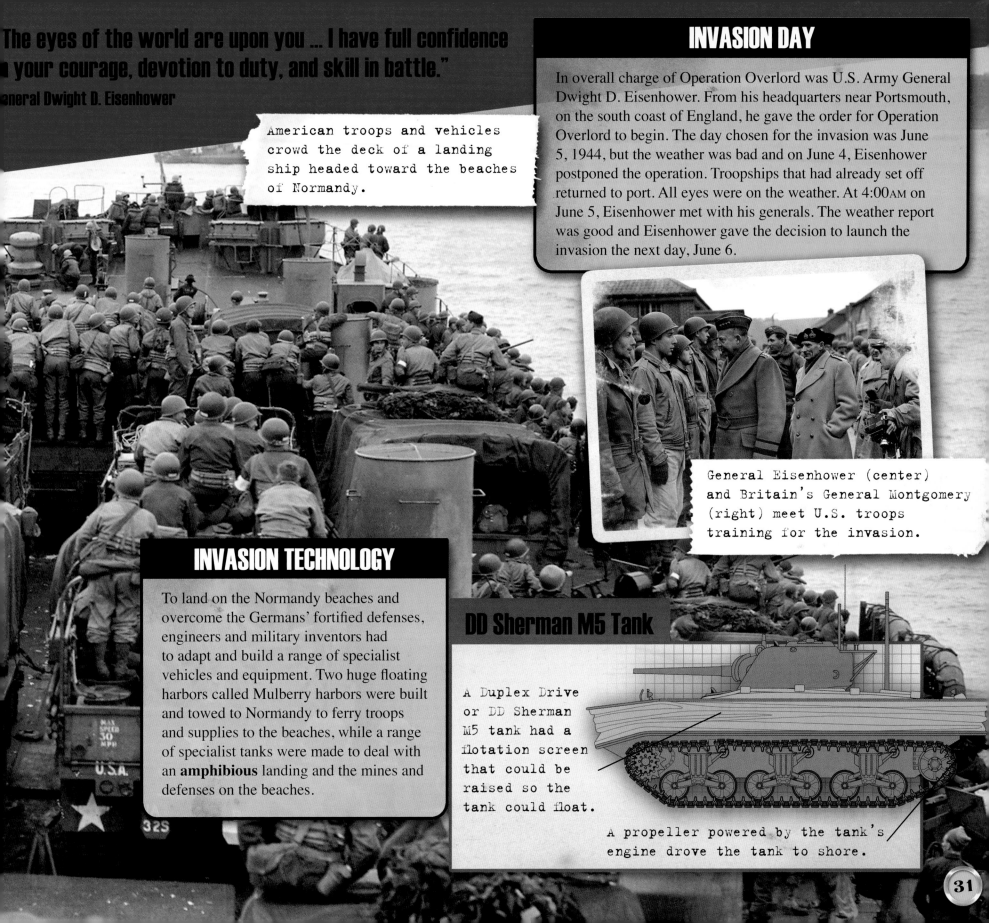

"The eyes of the world are upon you ... I have full confidence in your courage, devotion to duty, and skill in battle."
General Dwight D. Eisenhower

American troops and vehicles crowd the deck of a landing ship headed toward the beaches of Normandy.

INVASION DAY

In overall charge of Operation Overlord was U.S. Army General Dwight D. Eisenhower. From his headquarters near Portsmouth, on the south coast of England, he gave the order for Operation Overlord to begin. The day chosen for the invasion was June 5, 1944, but the weather was bad and on June 4, Eisenhower postponed the operation. Troopships that had already set off returned to port. All eyes were on the weather. At 4:00 AM on June 5, Eisenhower met with his generals. The weather report was good and Eisenhower gave the decision to launch the invasion the next day, June 6.

General Eisenhower (center) and Britain's General Montgomery (right) meet U.S. troops training for the invasion.

INVASION TECHNOLOGY

To land on the Normandy beaches and overcome the Germans' fortified defenses, engineers and military inventors had to adapt and build a range of specialist vehicles and equipment. Two huge floating harbors called Mulberry harbors were built and towed to Normandy to ferry troops and supplies to the beaches, while a range of specialist tanks were made to deal with an **amphibious** landing and the mines and defenses on the beaches.

DD Sherman M5 Tank

A Duplex Drive or DD Sherman M5 tank had a flotation screen that could be raised so the tank could float.

A propeller powered by the tank's engine drove the tank to shore.

D-DAY

After General Eisenhower gave the order for Operation Overlord to begin, a fleet of about 5,000 ships set out from ports along the south coast of England. They were heading for the beaches of Normandy. On board was an army of U.S., British, and Canadian troops, plus all the tanks, vehicles, fuel, and supplies they needed. The invasion was underway.

D-DAY BEGINS

The invasion fleet arrived off the Normandy coast late on June 5. Shortly after midnight, 23,400 U.S. and British paratroopers landed on French soil. The date—June 6, 1944—has gone down in history as "D-Day." The term is now used to refer to a day on which an important operation is to begin.

SAINTE-MÈRE-ÉGLISE

At 1:15AM, U.S. paratroopers landed in and around the village of Sainte-Mère-Église. Among them was paratrooper John Steele, whose parachute caught on the tower of the village church. He dangled there for two hours, pretending to be dead. He was captured by the defending Germans but later escaped. Many U.S. paratroopers died, but by 5:00AM the village was in U.S. hands—the first village in France to be liberated.

U.S. paratroopers watch for snipers as they advance through Sainte-Mère-Église.

BOMBARDMENT

At 5:30AM, Allied warships began bombarding the fortified German defenses along the coast. Added to this, some 9,000 airplanes, including USAAF Thunderbolts, Havocs, Marauders, and B-17 Flying Fortresses, dropped bombs on the German positions.

U.S. planes bomb German coastal defenses before the Normandy landings.

NORMANDY LANDINGS

At 6:30AM the first landing craft arrived. Back and forth they traveled between the troopships and the beaches, bringing ever more men ashore. Five beaches were used along a 60-mile stretch of the Normandy coast. U.S. troops came ashore at beaches codenamed "Utah" and "Omaha"; British and Canadian forces were landed at "Gold," "Juno," and "Sword."

The U.S. 1st Army unload vehicles and troops directly onto Omaha Beach after the landings on June 6.

Normandy Beaches, D-Day, June 6, 1944

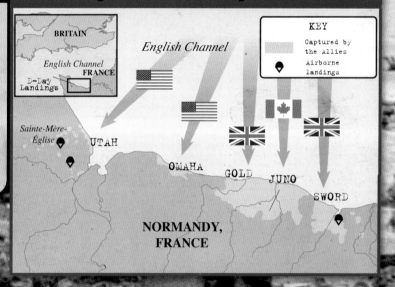

BRITAIN
English Channel
English Channel
FRANCE
D-Day Landings

KEY
Captured by the Allies
Airborne landings

English Channel

Sainte-Mère-Église

UTAH
OMAHA
GOLD
JUNO
SWORD

NORMANDY, FRANCE

FIGHTING ON THE BEACHES

The U.S. infantry on Utah Beach met with little resistance, but it was a different story farther along the coast on Omaha Beach. Here, German defenses were in commanding positions and U.S. forces came under heavy gunfire. About 3,000 U.S. soldiers died on Omaha Beach, but as thousands more came ashore they began to push the Germans back. By nightfall on D-Day, the Allies had landed around 73,000 U.S. and 83,000 British and Canadian troops in Normandy. The Allies had a foothold in France.

A view from a landing craft as troops wade toward Omaha Beach under fire.

THE BATTLE FOR FRANCE

Toward the end of July 1944, U.S., British, and Canadian forces were at full strength in Normandy. With their backs to the sea and the Germans penning them in, the next stage of the invasion was to punch a hole through enemy lines. Beyond lay the open countryside of France.

OPERATION COBRA

The U.S. plan to break out of Normandy was codenamed "Cobra." It began on July 25 with intensive bombing of German defenses. About 3,400 tons of bombs from U.S. bombers rained down onto a narrow section of the German **front**. The bombing opened up a gap in the German lines and U.S. ground forces poured through.

A Sherman tank advances through a bombed town during Operation Cobra.

LIBERATING PARIS

Under the command of General George Patton, the U.S. infantry advanced rapidly through northern France. Their goal was Paris, the French capital. Following an uprising by French resistance forces in the city, supported by a French armored division, the German opposition melted away. On August 25, French and U.S. forces entered Paris. After four years of German occupation, Paris was finally liberated.

U.S. troops are cheered by the crowds as they parade through Paris.

OPERATION DRAGOON

At the same time as U.S. forces were pushing the Germans out of northern France, the Allies invaded the south of France on August 15, 1944, in Operation Dragoon. The invasion was a success and U.S. forces advanced northward and the two armies joined up. However, the Allies now found it difficult to keep their rapidly advancing forces supplied with equipment, fuel, and food. The main push toward Germany slowed down and gave the retreating Germans time to regroup and plan a counterattack.

On September 11, 1944, General Patch's forces from the south joined up with General Patton's forces.

M4 Sherman Tank

U.S. M4 Sherman tanks faced larger German tanks with greater firepower during the offensive.

THE BATTLE OF THE BULGE

The German counterattack came in the Ardennes Forest, in Luxembourg and southern Belgium. They waited for bad weather, when Allied bomber planes would be grounded. At dawn on December 16, German forces unleashed a heavy artillery bombardment on U.S. positions. Thousands of German troops and hundreds of tanks then made a lightning advance, taking the U.S. troops by surprise. Within a week, the Germans had moved forward 50 miles, creating a "bulge" in the U.S. front line.

THE ALLIES STRIKE BACK

By December 23, the skies had cleared and the Allies were able to send airplanes to attack the advancing German forces. U.S. reinforcements arrived in the area and the German advance was halted and then pushed back. After three weeks of fighting, the "bulge" in the Allied lines had disappeared. The Battle of the Bulge, as it became known, was the largest and bloodiest battle fought by the U.S. in World War II. There were around 81,000 U.S. casualties, including 19,000 dead. The German forces suffered a devastating 100,000 casualties.

German troops pass a burning U.S. tank in the Ardennes.

GERMANY DEFEATED

By the spring of 1945, the German Army had retreated to Germany. It was caught between two advancing Allied forces: U.S. and British troops were pushing into Germany from the west, while Russian forces were advancing from the east. The battle for Germany became a race to take Berlin, the nation's capital.

U.S. troops scramble up the muddy banks of the Rhine after crossing by boat.

CROSSING THE RHINE

In western Germany, Allied forces advanced to the Rhine River. In a desperate effort to slow down the Allies, Hitler ordered the demolition of all the bridges across the Rhine. However, the bridge at Remagen escaped destruction. It was discovered by U.S. troops and on March 7, 1945, they began to cross the Rhine. By early April, thousands of Allied troops were crossing the river, using temporary **pontoon** bridges and boats. They closed in on Berlin. The German army was in full retreat, and many of its soldiers surrendered.

The 33rd President of the United States, Harry S. Truman.

A NEW PRESIDENT

As U.S. troops made rapid progress in Germany, sad news reached them from home. President Roosevelt had died suddenly, on April 12, 1945. For a short while, Hitler's hopes were raised. He hoped that the new president—President Harry S. Truman—would open peace talks with him. Hitler was wrong. President Truman, like President Roosevelt before him, demanded Germany's unconditional surrender.

HITLER'S LAST DAYS

U.S., British, and Russian forces pushed on to Berlin. The end was in sight and Hitler and his generals knew it. In the final days of the war, Hitler took refuge in an underground **bunker** in Berlin. It was here, on April 29, 1945, that he married his long-time companion, Eva Braun. That same day, Hitler discovered that some of his generals had gone behind his back and had decided to negotiate a cease-fire with the Allies. Hitler was furious. The next day, April 30, with the Russian army fighting, street by street, toward the bunker, Braun and Hitler killed themselves.

One of the last pictures of Hitler, giving medals to members of the Hitler Youth.

The Soviet flag being flown from the roof of the Reichstag.

BERLIN FALLS

The fighting in the east of Germany between German and Russian troops was bitter. Berlin was a city in ruins. Russian soldiers fought their way to the Reichstag building—the meeting place of the German parliament. Inside were 5,000 German fighters, determined to resist at all costs. Half of them died in the two days it took for the Russians to capture the building, room by room. Finally, on May 2, 1945, the Russian army controlled the Reichstag. Further resistance was pointless. Later that same day, German forces in Berlin surrendered to the Russians.

VICTORY IN EUROPE

On the day that Berlin fell, the fighting stopped in Italy when German troops surrendered to U.S. and British forces. Finally, on May 7, German generals agreed to a complete cease-fire. They traveled to the headquarters of Supreme Allied Commander General Dwight D. Eisenhower in Rheims, northern France. At 2:41AM on May 7, Germany signed the surrender document that would end the war in Europe. It was to take effect at one minute past midnight, May 8, 1945. On hearing the news, President Truman and Winston Churchill, the British prime minister, declared that May 8 should be celebrated as Victory in Europe Day (V-E Day).

A crowd celebrates V-E Day in Times Square, New York City.

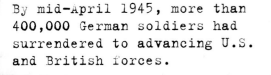

By mid-April 1945, more than 400,000 German soldiers had surrendered to advancing U.S. and British forces.

THE ISLAND CAMPAIGN

In May 1942, U.S. forces surrendered the Philippines to Japan. General Douglas MacArthur escaped to Australia, from where he declared, "I shall return." In 1944 he did just that, but first the U.S. had to take on the Japanese forces in the Pacific. In a series of hard-fought battles, infantry troops moved from island to island, edging closer to the ultimate goal—the islands of Japan.

BATTLE OF GUADALCANAL

On August 7, 1942, 19,000 U.S. troops landed on the island of Guadalcanal at the southern end of the Solomon Islands. Their mission had two purposes—to seize a newly built Japanese airfield and to prevent Japanese troops from landing on the island. It took six months of hard fighting in the island's steamy jungles and in naval battles around the island before Guadalcanal was finally in American hands. Some 7,000 U.S. and 31,000 Japanese troops had been killed, but it was a major U.S. victory.

U.S. GAINS IN THE PACIFIC

In June 1943, Operation Cartwheel started a major U.S. offensive in the Pacific. The first goal was to put out of action the Japanese military base at Rabaul on New Britain Island, New Guinea. The plan was then to move two great invasion forces toward the Philippines. In the southern Pacific, U.S. forces moved up through the Solomon Islands and New Guinea, pushing the Japanese back all the way. Then, in November 1943, U.S. forces moved into the central Pacific with assaults on the Marshall Islands and the Mariana Islands. The Marianas were taken in August 1944, following the battle of the Philippine Sea, where the U.S. Navy had devastated Japan's carrier fleet. Japan was now within striking distance of U.S. bombers and submarines.

U.S. troops fighting to take Buna, New Guinea, during Operation Cartwheel.

U.S. Marines come ashore from barges on a beach at Guadalcanal.

BATTLE OF LEYTE GULF

On October 20, 1944, U.S. forces arrived off the coast of Leyte in the Philippines—the starting point for the liberation of the islands. More than 200,000 soldiers landed on Leyte, and as General MacArthur waded ashore he announced: "People of the Philippines, I have returned." In the days that followed, the Battle of Leyte Gulf, the largest naval battle of modern times, was fought. The Japanese navy lost four aircraft carriers and 25 warships, despite sending a wave of suicide planes to save their fleet. Following this victory, it took U.S. forces until March 1945 to capture the Philippines.

The U.S. carrier *St. Lo* sank after a Japanese **kamikaze** plane dived into its flight deck during the Battle of Leyte Gulf.

Landing ships for tanks (LSTs) being unloaded during the Battle of Leyte.

Amphibian Tracked Vehicle

U.S. forces also used a range of **amphibian** tracked vehicles to deliver vehicles, troops, and supplies from ship to shore.

ISLAND LANDINGS

For the U.S. island campaign in the Pacific to succeed, vast numbers of men and vehicles had to be ferried from ships to the islands. They were moved by a fleet of landing ships, barges, and LCVPs (landing craft vehicle/personnel). General Eisenhower said that landing craft were one of the three vehicles that helped to win the war (the others were the Dakota transport plane and the jeep). Each landing craft had a flat bottom, so it could move through shallow water right up onto the beach.

ASSAULT ON JAPAN

Each Pacific island taken by U.S. forces brought them another step closer to Japan. The U.S. airforce boosted the Pacific War campaign by bombing Japanese cities and sinking ships transporting vital supplies. There was little or no opposition from Japan's military forces, yet the Japanese government showed no sign of surrendering.

BOMBING JAPAN

The Mariana Islands were the main base for USAAF operations against the home islands of Japan. Beginning in March 1945, the cities of Tokyo, Osaka, Yokohama, Nagoya, and Kobe were set alight by firebombs dropped at night. Tens of thousands of civilians perished and the cities were devastated. Far away in Europe, the war ended that May. Bombers were no longer needed there, so they were diverted to the bombing of Japan. The Japanese had never expected the war to come to their homeland and the raids caused widespread panic.

The ruins of Tokyo following the devastating firebombing.

B-29 SUPERFORTRESS

Many of the bombs that fell on Japan were dropped by the B-29 Superfortress. This heavy bomber carried up to 10 tons of bombs and had a range of 3,231 miles. It had a crew of 10, and was the biggest, fastest, and most modern bomber of the war.

SUBMARINE WARFARE

Japan needed to import oil, coal, rubber, and iron to keep its factories at work making supplies for the war. Rice was imported to keep the population fed. All this and more was brought to Japan by merchant ships. They were the country's lifeline. Just one week after the attack on Pearl Harbor, a U.S. submarine sank a Japanese merchant ship. The attacks increased and in 1944, U.S. submarines sank 2.7 million tons of Japanese ships loaded with cargo. The submarine campaign starved Japan of essential supplies.

USS *Barb* sank 17 enemy ships, including a Japanese carrier.

IWO JIMA

The tiny island of Iwo Jima, off the coast of Japan, saw bitter fighting between U.S. and Japanese forces in February and March 1945. Iwo Jima was heavily defended by the Japanese, who had laid minefields, set up machine-gun positions, and dug miles of tunnels. After five weeks of fighting, in which almost 7,000 U.S. troops died, and three times as many Japanese, Iwo Jima was taken.

U.S. Marines raise the American flag after the capture of Iwo Jima.

TAKING OKINAWA

Okinawa was the last stepping-stone before the main islands of Japan. On April 1, 1945, an invasion force of 172,000 U.S. troops landed on Okinawa. The Japanese were determined to fight to the last man, and kamikaze planes attacked U.S. ships. The conflict took almost three months and cost the lives of 15,000 U.S. and 130,000 Japanese troops. U.S. officials were now asking the question: "How many more have to die before Japan surrenders?"

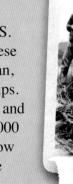

U.S. Marines capture Japanese troops hiding in a dugout.

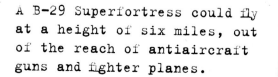

A B-29 Superfortress could fly at a height of six miles, out of the reach of antiaircraft guns and fighter planes.

ENDING THE WAR WITH JAPAN

The U.S. had planned to launch a large-scale invasion of Japan in November 1945. However, it was clear that many hundreds of thousands of troops would be lost on both sides. For this reason, the U.S. decided to use a new weapon—one with such power that it would force Japan to surrender and bring a quick end to the war.

Dr. Robert Oppenheimer, the project's chief scientist (center), and his team inspect the Trinity detonation site.

The atomic bomb for the Hiroshima mission, codenamed "Little Boy," weighed four tons but had the power of 20,000 tons of explosives.

THE MANHATTAN PROJECT

At about the same time as the Pearl Harbor attack in 1941, a secret project, codenamed "Manhattan Project," began. U.S. and British scientists worked around the clock to build an **atomic bomb** before their enemy. By 1945, they were ready to carry out a test explosion. The Trinity Test took place at dawn on July 16, 1945, at the Alamogordo bombing range, New Mexico. It was an awesome explosion of a type never seen before.

THE POTSDAM CONFERENCE

On July 17, the day after the Trinity Test, a conference began at Potsdam, Germany. Leaders of the U.S., Britain, and Russia talked about how to make Japan surrender. President Truman learned about the successful bomb test while he was there. On July 21, he gave the go-ahead for the atomic bomb to be used. He thought it would bring the war to a quick end and so save lives. Hiroshima was chosen as the target.

HIROSHIMA

On Monday, August 6, 1945, a B-29 bomber named *Enola Gay* took off, carrying an atomic bomb codenamed "Little Boy." At 8:15AM, the bomb was dropped on the Japanese city of Hiroshima. It exploded in the air over the city, killing 70,000 people in an instant. More deadly still was the radiation it produced—a lingering, invisible threat that continued to kill long after the explosion. In all, an estimated 200,000 people died.

The ruins of Hiroshima after the bomb. Ninety percent of the city's buildings were destroyed.

NAGASAKI

Nagasaki suffered the same fate as Hiroshima. On August 9, a B-29 bomber dropped the "Fat Man" atomic bomb onto the city. Some 75,000 people died when the bomb went off. Radiation sickness claimed more lives in the years that followed, and the death toll climbed to 150,000.

The "Fat Man" bomb that was dropped on Nagasaki.

General Yoshijiro Umezu of Japan signs the surrender on board the USS *Missouri*, watched by General Douglas MacArthur.

JAPAN SURRENDERS

The day before the bombing of Nagasaki, Russia declared war on Japan. Faced with an invasion by Russian forces, and with the U.S. using its super-bomb, Japan had no choice but to surrender, which it did on August 14, 1945. World War II was finally over, and the atomic bomb had changed the world forever.

AFTER THE WAR

World War II lasted almost six years and cost the lives of an estimated 80 million people. They had died in battle, in extermination camps, and from starvation and illness. Millions more were homeless or refugees. Towns and cities across the globe lay in ruins. The world at the end of 1945 was a very different place than it had been in 1939.

General MacArthur arriving to take up his post as the Supreme Allied Commander of the Occupation of Japan.

REBUILDING JAPAN

Days after Japan surrendered, General MacArthur arrived there. Thousands of U.S. troops occupied the country in a "peaceful invasion." For six years, from 1945 to 1951, MacArthur was in charge of running the U.S. occupation of Japan. He was based in Tokyo, the capital. During this time he helped to rebuild the economy of Japan. The country was transformed into a modern industrial nation. Japan went from being a dangerous enemy to one of the U.S.'s strongest allies.

GERMANY DIVIDED

After the war, Germany was divided into West and East Germany. The U.S., Britain, and France had control of West Germany (60 percent of the country), while Russia took control of East Germany. The capital, Berlin, was in the Russian zone and this was also divided. But tensions grew between Russia and its Western allies and in 1948, West Berlin was blockaded by the Russians, so the West had to fly in supplies.

TWO SUPERPOWERS

Two nations emerged from the war stronger and more powerful than before. They were the U.S. and Russia—and they became fierce rivals. Both were "superpowers" with influence across the world. They each wanted to outdo the other in an effort to become the world's leading nation. At first, only the U.S. had the ability to make an atomic bomb. But power shifted in 1949 when Russia tested an atomic bomb for the first time. From then on, these two superpowers began building up their stocks of weapons. A nuclear arms race had begun.

President Kennedy in the White House during the Cuban missile crisis: the closest the world has come to a nuclear war.

THE COLD WAR

As relations between the U.S. and Russia got frostier, a period of military tension began, which became known as the Cold War. For the next 40 years, until the early 1990s, neither side trusted the other. It was a period of great unease and there were times when it even seemed as if a conflict, or even a nuclear war, might begin—but thankfully it didn't.

Russia displays its nuclear missiles at a May Day parade in Moscow in 1961.

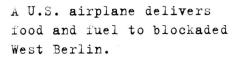

A U.S. airplane delivers food and fuel to blockaded West Berlin.

UNITED NATIONS

The war, and especially the use of the atomic bomb, had posed a threat to human civilization. It gave rise to the United Nations—an international organization whose job was to keep world peace. Efforts began even while the war was on. In June 1945, 51 nations were at the founding conference in San Francisco, and in October the United Nations, or U.N., was set up.

The headquarters of the United Nations in New York.

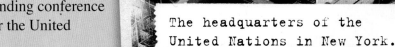

45

GLOSSARY

Allies
The countries at war against Germany
and Japan.

Amphibious
An amphibious landing involves delivering
troops and vehicles from ships onto land,
often involving amphibian vehicles that are
capable of traveling on both land and water.

Arsenal
A place where weapons and military
equipment are stored.

Atomic bomb
An immensely powerful explosive device in
which a great amount of energy is released
in a very short time.

Axis
The countries at war with the U.S., Britain,
and their allies.

Blitzkrieg
A German word meaning "lightning war,"
used to describe a rapid and successful
advance into enemy territory using the
combined power of warplanes and tanks.

Bunker
An underground shelter, reinforced with
steel and concrete.

Colony
A country or area under the political control
of another country.

Extermination camps
Camps where the Nazis imprisoned and
systematically killed Jews and other
prisoners. Also known as death camps.

Dictator
A person who rules a country with
absolute power.

Discrimination
When people are treated unfairly by others
because of their race, religion, gender, or
other characteristics.

Double agent
A spy who pretends to act for one country
but who really works for the enemy.

Front
A war zone: the place where the fighting
actually happens.

Führer
A German word meaning "leader," adopted
by Hitler as his official title in 1931.

Incendiary
A type of bomb designed to cause
a fire: a firebomb.

Infantry
Soldiers who fight on foot.

Kamikaze
Japanese suicide pilots who deliberately
crashed their airplanes into Allied ships.

Landing craft
A boat specially designed for landing troops
and military equipment on a beach.

Liberated
Freed from enemy occupation.

Morale
The confidence and discipline of a
person or a group of people at a
particular time.

Peninsula
A piece of land almost surrounded by water
or projecting out into a body of water.

Pontoon
A temporary bridge or floating landing stage.

Sonar
Stands for "sound navigation and ranging."
A system for the detection of objects
underwater.

Strategic
Carefully planned in order to serve
a particular purpose.

Torpedo
An underwater missile fired from
a submarine or an airplane.

Treaty
An agreement to do something,
made between countries or people.

INDEX

PICTURE CREDITS

The publishers would like to thank the following sources for their kind permission to reproduce the pictures in this book.

Key: t=top, l=left, r=right, c=centre, b=bottom.

AKG-Images: Ullstein Bild: 4 bl, 20 bl; Alamy: Interfoto: 28-29; Corbis: 10 cl, 23 bc, 44 bl; /Bettmann: 10-11, 15 bc, 15 tr, 20-21, 23 tl, 32 bl; /DPA: 36-37; /Hulton-Deutsch Collection: 20 c; Getty Images: 39 cr, 44-45; /AFP: 5 tr, 12bl; /Alinari: 7 tr; /American Stock: 11 br; /Bloomberg: 45 br; /Buyenlarge: 21 cr; /Fox Photos: 8-9; /FPG/Hulton Archive: 6 bl, 34-35; /A. E. French/Hulton Archive: 26 bl; /Galerie Bilderwelt: 30 c; /Gamma-Keystone: 26-27; /Hulton Archive: 19 cr; /Keystone: 7 bl, 12-13, 14 bl, 20 bc, 27 br, 37 tr, 38 bl; /Keystone-Gamma: 42 c, 43 cr; /Photo12/UIG: 35 tr, 36bl; /Popperfoto: 24 cl, 27 tr, 31 r, 34 bl, 43 br; /Roger Viollet Collection: 6-7, 7 br, 13 tc, 25 tr, 25 cr, 30 bl; /Sovfoto/UIG: 21tr, 37 cr, 45 l; /Time & Life Pictures: 8 cl, 22 cl, 22-23, 24-25, 38-39, 39 t, 42 bl, 45 cr; Reg Manning/Arizona Republic: 8 bc; Imperial War Museums, London: (MH 11040) 4-5, (A 23977) 30-31, (EA 26941) 32-33, (EA 48015) 35 br, (M 29427) 43 tr; Library of Congress, Prints and Photographs Division: 29 br, 36 c; National Archives and Records Administration, Washington D.C.: 11 cl, 16, 16-17, 17, 18, 18-19, 19 br, 33 bc, 41 c, 41 br, 42-43; Press Association Images: 37 bc, 40 bl; Private Collection: 23 tr; Topfoto.co.uk: 13 bl, 13 cr; /The Granger Collection: 14-15, 23 c, 25 br; Jon Mitchell: 28 bl; U.S. Department of Defense: 40-41; Courtesy of ussubvetsofworldwarii.org: 41 t; Wiki Commons: 9 r, 22 bc;

Every effort has been made to acknowledge correctly and contact the source and/or copyright holder of each picture and Carlton Books Limited apologises for any unintentional errors or omissions, which would be corrected in future editions of this book.

This edition published by Scholastic Inc., 557 Broadway, New York, NY 10012, by arrangement with Carlton Books.

10 9 8 7 6 5 4 3 2 1
ISBN: 978-0-545-64886-8
Printed in Dongguan, China.

Senior Editor: Paul Virr
Senior Art Editor: Jake da'Costa
Military History Consultant: Dr Allan R. Millett
Maps: MW Digital Graphics, Martin Brown
Cover Design: Jake da'Costa
Illustrations: Peter Liddiard
Picture Research: Ben White
Production: Ena Metagic